An Audience with Jesus

By
Rev. Msgr. John F. Davis

ST. PAUL EDITIONS

NIHIL OBSTAT:
　Rev. Richard V. Lawlor, S.J.
　Censor

IMPRIMATUR:
　✠Humberto Cardinal Medeiros
　Archbishop of Boston

Excerpts from the English translation of *The Roman Missal* © 1973, International Committee on English in the Liturgy, Inc. All rights reserved.

Photos: DSP

ISBN 0-8198-0721-4 cloth
　　　0-8198-0722-2 paper

Copyright © 1982, by the Daughters of St. Paul

Printed in the U.S.A. by the Daughters of St. Paul
50 St. Paul's Ave., Boston, MA 02130

The Daughters of St. Paul are an international congregation of religious women serving the Church with the communications media.

*Especially for my parents
Frank and Amelia
and for
all who taught me
to love the Eucharist*

CONTENTS

Foreword	11
The Eucharist and I	13
The Eucharist as Center	21
The Eucharist as Solace	29
The Eucharist and the Virgin	37
The Eucharist and Unity	43
The Eucharist and Devotion	51
The Eucharist and Transubstantiation I	57
The Eucharist and Transubstantiation II	65
The Eucharist and Cardinal Newman	73
The Eucharist as Sacrament and Sacrifice	81
The Eucharist and Pope John Paul II	89
The Eucharist and Holy Thursday	97
The Eucharist and the Priest	105
The Eucharist and Our Brethren	113
The Eucharist and the Four Ends of Prayer	121
The Eucharist—Holy Communion	129

Foreword

Perhaps I have attempted too much when I have undertaken to write a book about the Eucharist.

I have wanted to write such a book for a long time. Now I feel it is more needed than previously. The present spiritual emphasis on human beings and personal charisms has perhaps detracted from devotion to the Eucharistic Christ.

Of course, I do not encroach on the field of the scholar or the theologian. This is simply a recollection of and compilation of Eucharistic devotion from long ago until now. The facets of this incredible mystery all contribute to the realization of this triumph of Jesus' love.

The book is intended for those who desire Eucharistic devotion, including those not of our Catholic Faith.

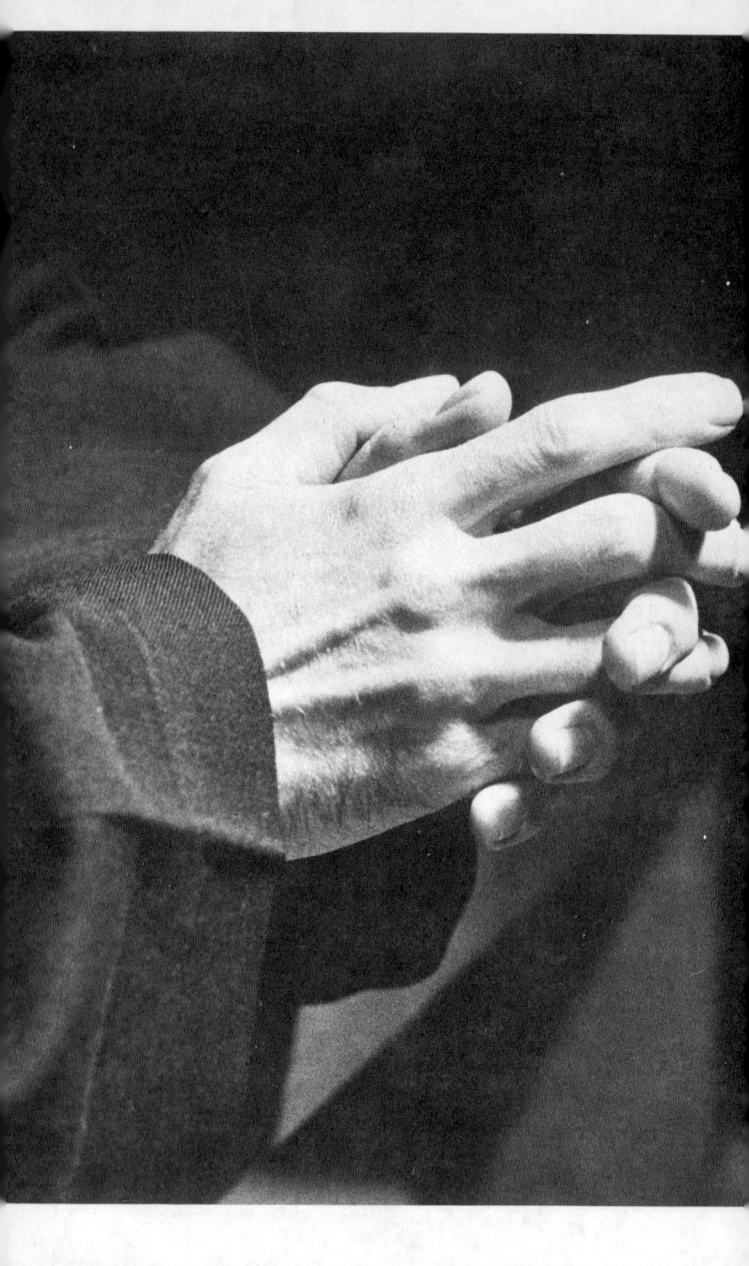

*The
Eucharist
and I*

I received my First Holy Communion on the 26th of May, 1929—I was nine years old and four months. That day is still in my clear recollection. Admittedly I was older than most of our first communicants today, and I cannot help but consider that an advantage. The impression was firm and more lasting.

I received the Eucharist for the first time with a small group of children, perhaps twenty in number. I remember none of them, perhaps because I regarded it as a singular event and experience. It was as though the Lord was coming only to me in the history of the world.

The church of my First Holy Communion was very small, old, and simple, dedicated to Our Lady of Sorrows. The church has been demolished and replaced. To me, however, it was majestic and the gate of heaven. It was St. Peter's in Rome, although I did now know of that basilica at all then.

Entirely taught by one dynamic, hard-working, selfless nun, we had a long preparation for that day. Sister came to our church from another part of the city. She traveled each Sunday by bus, and I can see her as if it were yesterday, walking from the bus to our church hall. She always carried a briefcase. She attended Mass with us each Sunday at 8:00 a.m. and then we had our instruction. After that she returned by bus to her convent. It was an hour's trip each way. Now I realize that she was fasting from midnight until near midday and with no apparent second thought of her difficult schedule. I wrote to her for many years until my ordination and then for some twenty years more. She was an important part of the Holy Communion and personal preparation. I remember her well.

The day of First Communion was definitely the most important day of my life. We were imbued with that idea; we believed it firmly.

My First Confession was the day before my First Communion and we were well prepared. The priest seemed very old to me (I don't know whether he was) and he spoke very broken English. He asked me very pertinent questions and I answered them directly. I thought it was supposed to be that way.

I was completely in awe of the Eucharist as I received our Lord for the first time. That afternoon I had my picture taken by my father on one of the few grass lawns in our neighborhood. It was a good photo and I have it till today.

I don't recall whether I became a communicant each Sunday then, but I became a daily communicant about three years later, how or why I don't exactly know. Only God would know that. Knowing my own unworthiness and weakness, I felt from that time a daily need for the Blessed Sacrament.

So, you see, we had no elaborate program of First Penance and First Communion. Nor did we dream of going to Communion without going to confession each Saturday night. There were very long lines at the confessionals, and the priests who heard confession were very conscientious, very kind, and very concerned. It was an unbelievably important school of spiritual growth, although we were completely unaware of all the attendant circumstances—it was simply the way God wanted it to be.

It is all quite different now. We could not possibly have been given more love of the Eucharist.

*O Jesus, present in the Blessed Sacrament,
keep me in awe of
Your Holy Presence in the Eucharist,
as I was on the day
of my First Holy Communion,
when I could not possibly
have been given more love for You.*

*The
Eucharist
as Center*

"No one can do great things for God who has not spent much time alone with God in prayer."

With these words we were reminded that we must be Eucharistic priests if we were going to be effective priests. Our lives were to be centered in the Eucharist.

Could it be that today with our great emphasis on Christ in persons, we have forgotten Christ in the Eucharist? Our churches are becoming empty of adorers. The great churches of the large cities and the smaller churches of towns and villages always found people worshiping the Eucharistic God. It is not so today—many of the churches today are quite wanting of those seeking Jesus in Eucharistic prayer.

St. John Vianney, the Curé d'Ars, found much of his strength in long hours of prayer on his knees before the Sacrament. They say that Mother Teresa of Calcutta will not take on a mission for her sisters unless they have a chapel with the Eucharist present at all times. Also, her sisters spend the first hours of each day in prayer before the Eucharist so that they will have the strength to carry out the apostolate each day among the poorest of the poor. We all know how persistently during his life Fulton J. Sheen urged the daily holy hour and how he himself prepared his sermons in the presence of the Eucharist.

The source of the strength of the present Holy Father, Pope John Paul II, is our Lord in the Eucharist. I have read that the very best representation of the Holy Father is of him kneeling humbly in prayer before the Blessed Sacrament. This is the way I most often think of the Pope, kneeling and praying with his head on the shoulder of the Eucharistic Christ, begging help for the needs of the Church. This is the way the Pope prays. Can we do otherwise? He refers in his sermons to "our Eucharistic Jesus" and becomes most eloquent when he finds in the Eucharist "a God who breathes, lives and acts" (Paul Claudel). How impressive it was that whenever the Pope entered the great cathedrals in Boston, New York, Chicago, and Washington on his visit to our country, he would immediately seek out the altar of the Eucharist, kneel before the Real Presence of Christ, and pray—holding his hands to his head, bowed humbly in prayer.

Obviously the Holy Father combines a life of great activity with long hours of prayer. The soul of his apostolate is Eucharistic prayer. Social action is useless unless preceded by prayer before the Eucharist. The vertical direction to God must precede the horizontal thrust to men. Perhaps this needs to be reemphasized. Are not the cloisters of our contemplatives the powerhouses of prayer that give success to the active apostolate? We dare not disconnect the source lest we effect a spiritual energy crisis.

The whole Church takes strength from the fact that the Pope kneels at his *prie-dieu* each night. He is praying in the presence of the Eucharistic God. From the reliance of the Pope on the Eucharistic God, even the prodigal son can take courage to lay his head on the shoulder of the Father. The Eucharist is essential for our Faith to take substance and form. That is why the Holy Father carried the Blessed Sacrament through the streets of Rome in the Corpus Christi procession of 1979 for the first time in ten years. The Pope was telling the world to seek Christ in the

Eucharist first and foremost, and to cling to His Presence in mind and heart.

Wherever he travels, this Pope celebrates the Eucharist before thousands, reminding us that the principal means of sustenance is the action of the Eucharist. This will be his continued style even now after the attempted assassination of May 13, 1981. He will dramatize in this sense the sixth chapter of St. John's Gospel. He will feed the multitude with the Bread of Heaven. This Pope has helped us to find Jesus in the Eucharist. He refers to the Eucharist as "an audience with Jesus."

He knows that from that audience we depart with credentials of new strength—much the same strength that our Lady and the Apostles had when they came down from Calvary.

O Jesus, present in the Blessed Sacrament, remain the center of my life, the source of my strength. Keep me seeking You first and foremost; let me cling to Your Presence in mind and heart.

*The
Eucharist
as Solace*

I have read that St. Francis of Assisi, though an Italian, loved France because the Eucharist was more venerated there than in any other country of the world. The time of that saint was a worldly and irreligious time as it is now. Yet it was a time in which the honor of the Eucharist was more prevelant, increasingly so from century to century. It seemed that the Eucharistic life of Christ was developing as did the human life of Christ. Jesus' life unfolded and expanded to infinite glory. The Eucharist should unfold and give life and glory to the Church.

In the humblest church, it is the Eucharist that gives life and meaning to that Church community. Simply, quietly, without music or lights or fanfare, Jesus is there. Only the small lamp of the sanctuary reminds us of the Real Presence. Where the Eucharist is not present, there is no warmth or life. "The Lord is taken away." The Catholic churches welcome the stranger; you are at home at once because God in the Blessed Sacrament welcomes you.

I remember once in my life being quite alone in a large, a very large, eastern city of our country. Instinctively I sought out the Eucharist in one of the churches. That night there were many others there in silent prayer before the Real Presence of Christ in the sacrament of the altar. Believe me, we were joined in Christ; none of us was alone. This was solace and refuge for us, joined in this Eucharistic faith. I doubt seriously whether this same event could occur today for many reasons, one of which is this: I genuinely wonder whether the young generation's faith in the Eucharist is that strong, that active, that deeply rooted. Perhaps I am wrong. I hope so.

At Lourdes, even Mary has stepped aside to make way for Christ. There is no place in the world where Christ in the Eucharist is more glorified. The procession of the Eucharist by candlelight is the highpoint of each day. Here the pilgrims are joined in faith, and all the countries of the world are united as the procession winds from the grotto to show that Jesus is the Gift of the Virgin Mary. Now she stands at the side of her Son so that He may console.

The Eucharist in our churches and in our shrines creates a world of its own. It breathes an atmosphere of faith, love, hope and hospitality. Most of us who do not live sheltered lives find ourselves between the noisy, worldly, excited environment in which we are forced to live and the peaceful presence of the Eucharist. The Eucharist obliges us worldlings to build for ourselves an inner retreat, an underground refuge. We have lost much ground. As the poet says, "the world is too much with us." We have forgotten the necessity for the delicate balance, and the noise has consumed us. We can retrace our steps, I suppose, if we get rid of all that distracts us from Christ. There are too many plans and programs and directives I would think. When Pius X was asked his program, he pointed to the cross and said, "That is my program." So the Eucharist is our program, our directive. We must tear down the walls that have estranged us from the prayer of the Eucharist in our churches to bring Christ near to us. That humility should overcome every obstacle.

> "Everything is silent. Do come, night of mine!
> Come hither, intangible shelter!
> Come sacred nuptial silence!

Sun of my soul, come peace! Come friendship!
Come abundance!
Come with me, come, my God, come Ardent repose!"

                        Paul Claudel

Claudel has caught that evening in the large church in the large city where I, quite alone, sought the Eucharistic Christ and found not only Him but my brother. Claudel had the same experience when on Christmas Day, 1886, at the age of eighteen, going through the familiar spiritual crisis which seems to be the hazard of youth, he suddenly walked into Notre Dame Cathedral in Paris and emerged transformed: "and then suddenly that event occurred which dominated my life. In a single instant my heart was touched and I believed." Until his death that Eucharistic faith dominated his whole life—it animated him—it was his life. Claudel had no choice but to accept and absorb his God.

There are many who would find the presence of Christ in our churches, in the tabernacle. He would be "ardent repose," "sacred nuptial silence," "intangible shelter," "sun of my soul," "abundance." Seldom has it been put more beautifully by one who has found Christ than Claudel did at age eighteen—so young!

O Jesus, present in the Blessed Sacrament in our churches, You give us solace and refuge; You give us faith, hope, love and hospitality. You build for us an inner retreat, an ardent repose. Help us to seek You and find You in the tabernacle.

The Eucharist and the Virgin

One of my favorite titles of the Blessed Virgin Mary is Our Lady of the Most Blessed Sacrament. The body of Christ was brought forth by the Virgin Mary—why should she not be known by that title? The veneration paid to Mary would certainly accompany the cult of the Eucharist. There is no strain between these two aspects; rather, one reinforces the other. As we have mentioned in a previous chapter, at Lourdes Mary steps aside for her Eucharistic God. In many instances what has begun as devotion to Mary leads to the worship of the Eucharist. It seems that anyone who loves the Mother is led to the Son. His Mother prays for us and Christ finds us waiting for Him. *"Ad Jesum per Mariam."* "To Jesus through Mary." The Mother of God stands at the foot of the cross as we struggle up the hill of our own Calvary.

The Virgin Mother of God seems to be absent through the long hours of her

Son's misery and desolation in the early stages of the passion. Otherwise He would not have felt so abandoned. She would have been present to comfort Him. It is not until the scene of the crucifixion that she appears, to stand by Him as the Son of God is lifted up between heaven and earth.

However, the time after the ascension finds her seated in the cenacle with the Apostles (Acts 1:14). In Acts we read that the new Church was persevering "in the communion of the breaking of the bread." Mary's was the joy of the standing *"juxta crucem,"* "beside the cross," but also hers was the comfort of receiving her Son in Holy Communion from the first priests of the newly-established Church. She became for the second time a living ciborium, carrying her Son close to her heart. Jesus Himself drew this comparison of His presence in the Virgin and in the hearts of the beloved. Once, when about to receive the sacred Host, St. Gertrude asked, "What gift are You going to grant me?" And the Lord Jesus Himself answered, "The gift of my whole being with my divine nature, as formerly my Virgin Mother received it." So the Virgin leads us to Jesus each day of our lives.

Mary stands in the midst of the Church as she stood at the foot of the cross.

The coat of arms of John Paul II is a beautiful manifestation of the closeness of Mary to the Eucharist. The main representation is the cross, whose form does not correspond to the customary heraldic model. The vertical bar of the cross is unusually long and beside it is a majestic capital letter "M." This is placed under the horizontal bar of the cross, recalling the presence of Mary beneath the cross and her singular participation in the redemption. She is the Mother of the Redeemer. She is Our Lady of the Most Blessed Sacrament. With Mary we love the Lord Jesus present in the Eucharist. "He is present in a sacrificial way in holy Mass which renews the sacrifice of the cross. To go to Mass means going to Calvary to meet Him, our Redeemer" (Pope John Paul II). Such a beautiful reminder from the Pope of Mary!

Our Lady of the Blessed Sacrament, you gave us the body and blood of Jesus, the gift of His whole being with His divine nature; now graciously lead us to Jesus every day of our lives: to Jesus through Mary.

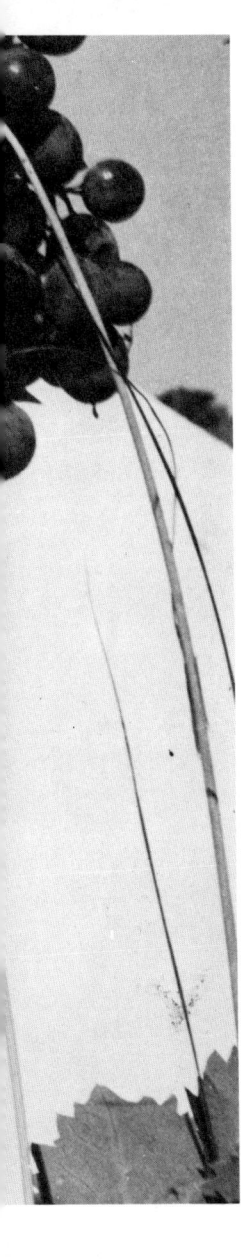

The Eucharist and Unity

"The spiritual life is not confined to participation in the liturgy. The Christian is assuredly called to pray with his brethren, but he must also pray to the Father in secret.... He should pray without ceasing" (Vatican II, *Constitution on the Sacred Liturgy*).

"The way to nourish faith is by prayer before the tabernacle....

"There is sometimes encountered nowadays the idea that somehow devotion to the Real Presence in the tabernacle is less stressed than it was formerly and that it is somehow less than strictly liturgical. This is very foolish" (Most Rev. Cahal B. Daly, Bishop of Ardagh, Ireland).

It would be a pity if all the worthwhile activity in which we are engaged so gainfully suddenly became a house of cards. The concert could go flat if the performers have not bothered to tune their instruments. As Fr. Raoul Plus, S.J., reminds us in one of his meditations, the only real danger is the loss of the tabernacle key.

What need is there to tell our troubles to others? To ruminate our miseries? Jesus in the tabernacle is eager to receive us and to help us. Devotion to the Blessed Sacrament is the Mass prolonged, held in meditation; indeed, it makes the liturgy more personal, more thankful, less routine, less mechanical.

The Eucharist is the driving force of the liturgy. There is no other way. Chesterton, that enthusiast of heaven, calls the Mass "The Thing." Our daily lives are spent in union with the Holy Sacrifice of the Mass. That is our daily offering in the apostolate.

We are particularly aware of the unity aspect of the Eucharist. Through the Eucharist, we are continually drawn into unity with Jesus and with one another. The liturgy of the Mass continually reminds us by the use of the vernacular and by hymns that "it is good and pleasant for us to dwell in unity." It is a sacrifice of unity wherein we pray for our brothers and sisters who are united with the apostles and martyrs throughout the ages. It is the wellspring for far more universal unity among all Christians. The Eucharist could be the triumph of the ecumenical spirit bringing all to our Faith.

This was instanced when some 1,400 Protestant and Catholic youths met at TAIZE in September, 1960. On the final day, after having prayed together, they requested to be allowed to participate in a single Eucharistic Celebration. These youths desired that unity which only the Eucharist could effect. Fr. Roger Schultz, Protestant Prior of TAIZE, himself an ardent ecumenist, realized that it was unthinkable to allow intercommunion of the Eucharist. The reason was simple. Common worship and prayer, though a sign of the desire for unity, cannot be a sign if there is not unity of belief. Communion would then be a false sign, since it only pointed to disunity of belief.

The Holy Spirit will remove the obstacles to unity, the object of our Eucharistic prayer. This private prayer is personal but it unites us with all our brothers in the Lord. It develops the Christian personality for the Christian life of the liturgy. It prepares us for Mass and it flows from the Mass. It prepares us to join with others in the liturgy by deepening our union with our Lord.

O Jesus, present in the Blessed Sacrament, in Your Sacred Presence all creatures of God are joined. Draw us continually into unity with Yourself and with one another. It is good for us to dwell together in unity; remove the obstacles to unity in our Christian Faith.

The Eucharist and Devotion

"We beseech you to foster devotion to the Eucharist which should be the focal point and the goal of all other forms of devotion" (Pope Paul VI, *Mysterium Fidei*).

The above quote must be our constant effort to realize devotion as part of our lives. It is the desire of Jesus Christ and of His Church to see us approach the Sacred Banquet every day with a pure mind. There is no better way to offer thanks for such a gift as the Eucharist. So many people try with so much personal effort to attend Mass each day. It means everything to them. I have arranged in our parish church to have Mass celebrated each day at noon—so as to allow greater attendance. For many who are in the offices nearby it is a great convenience at the lunch hour. For many who are getting a bit older it is so much easier than an earlier hour—especially when you have to walk. For many "it is their highpoint of the day." They all draw strength from the

Eucharist and many stay long after the Mass is completed to prolong their Eucharistic adoration and devotion.

The Eucharist conquers the passions, and washes away lesser sins that are the results of human frailty. The visit to the sacramental Presence is a proof of gratitude to God. It is a pledge of love, an act of adoration owed to Christ our Lord present there. He is in the midst of us day and night. He dwells in us "with the fullness of grace and truth" (cf. Jn. 1:14).

Anyone who has true devotion to the Eucharist appreciates and understands how precious is a life hidden with Christ in God, "by whom all things are and by whom we exist" (1 Cor. 8:6). The Eucharist fosters a social love, meaning that our devotion flows over to the cause of the community. We put the common good ahead of the private good. For those who are devoted to the Eucharist there develops an ecclesial spirit born of that devotion. We begin to live in the presence of God. That becomes a reality. "Through Him, with Him, and in Him," and then for others. "His eye is on the sparrow"—therefore, it is on me. Every act, every decision is born of this devotion and is nourished by it.

From this comes the fourfold Eucharistic prayer—adoration, reparation, thanksgiving and petition. All designed to bring us closer to our Eucharistic God.

I adore the Father
I have offended the Father
I thank You, loving Father
I "go to" the Father
—many times each day.

"We can hardly bear to leave that Fatherly shoulder to which the prodigal son returned in tears" (Paul Claudel).

I cannot imagine a more beautiful way to think of our Eucharistic God than "that Fatherly shoulder." How better evoke the presence of God and express devotion?

All this is to say that the presence of Christ in the Eucharist gives us a destination and the joyful hope of attaining it—if only we are devoted!

O Jesus, present in the Blessed Sacrament, devotion to Your Real Presence conquers the passions and washes away lesser sins which result from human frailty.
Devotion to You is a pledge of love and helps us to find how precious is a life hidden with Christ in God.

*The Eucharist
and
Transubstantiation I*

"We confess that the body of the Lord was given with His own hands to the disciples, entirely to all and entirely to each" (St. Thomas Aquinas).

No theologian explains transubstantiation better than the Angelic Doctor, St. Thomas Aquinas. He is the greatest exponent of the doctrine of the Eucharist. Whoever receives our Lord in the Eucharist receives the entire person of Christ: body, blood, soul, humanity, divinity. To try to ponder this mystery we have to return to the statement of our Lord at the Last Supper: "This is my body. This is my blood." The Lord here does not use a comparison or a parable. He speaks directly and affirmatively. The only emphasis that might break the flow of the words is on the word "my." It is the body and blood of the Lord. "This is *my* body. This is *my* blood."

These words are precise, strong and powerful, with no indirection. It is His body and it is His blood. We have to accept these words without reservation. We have to believe in the authority and power behind these words—the authority and power of God. The words are simple words so that there will be no misunderstanding, making it easier for faith to pierce the clouds. Even Luther remained unshaken in his belief and wrote on his desk with a piece of chalk *"Hoc est corpus meum,"* "This is my body," as he became angry with the doctrine of Zwingli which held the usual Protestant interpretation: "This is the symbol of...." Luther did not hold, however, that the Real Presence was effected by the words of the priest. We know that God works through the priest in accomplishing the miracle of transubstantiation as the bread and wine are changed into the body and blood of Christ. The substances of the bread and wine become the body and blood of Christ. The "accidents" of color, taste, appearance do not change. The substance is changed or transformed and becomes really and truly the body and blood of Jesus Christ.

I would not think that this doctrine of the Eucharist depends entirely upon this scholastic distinction of Thomistic philosophy. Nor should this doctrine be exclusively confined to the language or structures of St. Thomas Aquinas. But no one has better explained this doctrine. Nor has anyone written more eloquently in praise of the Sacrament:

> "O Godhead hid, devoutly I adore Thee,
> Who truly are within the forms before me;
> To Thee my heart I bow with bended knee,
> As failing quite in contemplating Thee.
> Sight, touch, and taste in Thee are each deceived;
> The ear alone most safely is believed:
> I believe all the Son of God has spoken
> Than Truth's own word there is no truer token!"

No one has ever surpassed the Eucharistic prayer of St. Thomas. Christ has put His seal upon him. As M. Jacques Maritain states: "At Paris when the masters sought his advice as to the proper method of teaching the Eucharist, he first went and laid his answer on the altar, imploring the crucifix; brethren who were watching suddenly saw Christ standing in front of him on the draft which he had written and heard these words: 'Thou hast written well concerning the Sacrament of my body and blood and thou hast well and truthfully resolved the problem which has been put to thee, so far as it is possible to be known on earth and described in human words.'" This belief of St. Thomas pervaded his whole being until that last moment when he received Viaticum and testified to the Eucharistic God that his whole life had been one of complete prayer and study, preaching and teaching the Real Presence. And then he added, "If I have done anything ill, I leave it to the correction of the Roman Church. In that obedience I depart from this life."

The Eucharist had been the essence of St. Thomas' life, the very food of his journey to God. The Eucharist is not a reward; it is medicine and food for our journey. Once we accept the transubstantiation doctrine, we are urged to receive our Lord each day. No temptation is so great as to separate us from the daily reception of the Sacred Host. When everything seems worst, it is precisely then that we need the Lord most. It is no wonder that the Popes have urged frequent, if not daily, Communion to withstand the temptations of the times. With confidence and without worry, we approach the Sacred Banquet with the army of those who have preceded us and we hear the words first addressed to St. Francis de Sales: "I am not called 'He who condemns'; my name is Jesus." "This is my body. This is my blood."

O Jesus, present in the Blessed Sacrament, "we confess that the body of the Lord was given with His own hands to the disciples, entirely to all and entirely to each."

"O Godhead hid, devoutly I adore Thee."

*The Eucharist
and
Transubstantiation II*

Here a caution must be added about certain theologians who would explain the Lord's Presence in the Eucharist through the term "transignification." This is a theory with a new title but it could be the heresy of Calvin in the 16th century and Berengarius in 1079. Berengarius was the first who dared deny the Eucharistic change.

Transignification means that the bread and wine take on a new meaning at Mass. It says the "significance" of the bread and wine has changed in that the bread and wine when used in the Eucharist must be treated differently from ordinary table bread and wine. They must, they say, be treated with respect and reverence since the "significance" is now associated with the Eucharist—not just with an ordinary usage such as at the dinner table. Now it "represents" the Lord's body, they say.

It does not "represent"! We say, "It is!"

In St. Paul's first epistle to the Corinthians 11:27 we read, "Anyone who eats the bread and drinks the cup of the Lord unworthily will be guilty of desecrating the body and blood of the Lord." At the Last Supper, Jesus states absolutely and not in metaphor: "This is my body." The Church has always held that after the consecration what looks like bread (the accidents) remains; the actual bread (the substance) has been replaced by the substance of the body of the Lord. It is the same with the substance of the wine becoming the substance of the blood and the appearance remaining.

Pope Gregory VII stated this clearly in 1079 in the following oath: "I believe in my heart and profess with my lips that the bread and wine which are placed upon the altar are, by the mystery of the sacred prayers and words of the Redeemer, substantially changed into the true and life-giving flesh and blood of Jesus Christ our Lord and that after the consecration, there is present the true body of Christ which was born of the Virgin and—offered for the salvation of the world—hung on the cross and now sits at the right hand of the Father; and that there is present the true blood of Christ which flowed from His side. They are present not only by means of a sign and of the efficacy of the sacrament, but also in the very reality and truth of their nature and substance."

This is the original sweeping renunciation (1079) of transignification. This is not new theory but old error revisited. The oath of Pope Gregory VII excludes all possible misunderstanding. At the Last Supper Jesus meant exactly what He said.

Paul VI, that saintly Pontiff, states in *Mysterium Fidei:* "Nor is it allowable to discuss the mystery of transubstantiation without mentioning what the Council of Trent stated about the marvelous conversion of the whole substance of the bread into the body and of the whole substance of the wine into the blood of Christ, speaking rather only of what is called 'transignification' and 'transfinalization.'"

Everyone can see that the spread of such an opinion does great harm to the faith as well as to devotion to the divine Eucharist. In this connection, Paul VI tells us that he has the duty to warn us of the "grave danger" involved for correct faith. The reason is clear; the Eucharist contains Christ Himself and it is "a kind of perfection of the spiritual life; in a way it is the goal of all the sacraments" (Saint Thomas).

Theodore of Mopsuestia, quoted by Paul VI in *Mysterium Fidei,* addressed these very explicit words to the faithful: "The Lord did not say, 'This is a symbol of my body, and this is a symbol of my blood,' but 'This is my body. This is my blood.' We look not at the nature of those things which lie before us and are perceived by the senses, for by the prayer of thanksgiving and the words spoken over them, they have been changed into flesh and blood."

Faith in Christ our Lord present in the Sacrament of the Eucharist by transubstantiation must therefore be preserved in "purity and integrity—a faith which seeks only to remain perfectly loyal to the word of Christ and of the Apostles and unambiguously rejects all erroneous and mischievous opinions" *(Mysterium Fidei).*

May we here, in conclusion, be grateful for the Encyclical letters which I have frequently quoted, that of Pope Paul VI, *Mysterium Fidei* (September 3, 1965), and the letter of Pope John Paul II to all the bishops, *On the Mystery and Worship of the Eucharist,* entitled *Dominicae cenae* (February 24, 1980). These have been the source material of this important caution in connection with this doctrine which is at the heart and center of our religion.

*O Jesus, truly present in the
Sacrament of the Last Supper,
guard us against revisiting
old errors that would diminish
our appreciation of the mystery
of transubstantiation,
the mystery of our Faith.*

The Eucharist and Cardinal Newman

Cardinal Newman became a Catholic because of his reading of the Fathers of the Church, and he was greatly attracted by the teaching of the Church on the Holy Eucharist. Shortly before Newman's reception into the Church, a friend said: "Think about what you are doing. If you become a Catholic, you will lose your income of four thousand pounds sterling." Newman answered: "What are four thousand pounds compared to one Holy Communion?" Cardinal Newman did not conform himself to those about him; his faith impelled him to do otherwise. That faith was essentially centered in the Eucharist. His writings on the Eucharist best show the greatness of his conversion. Some of these writings follow.

He says, "To me nothing is so consoling, so piercing, so thrilling as the Mass.... I could attend Mass forever and not be tired." This is perhaps the premise of his life: the supreme consolation that the Mass was for him, the thrill without ending.

He describes the Eucharistic Presence: "Thou dwellest on our altars. Thou the most Holy, the most High, in light inaccessible, and angels fall down before Thee there; and out of visible substances and forms Thou choosest what is choicest to represent and hold Thee. The finest wheat-flour, and the purest wine, are taken as the outward symbols; the most sacred and majestic words minister to the sacrificial rite; altar and sanctuary are adorned decently or splendidly, as our means allow; and Thy priests perform their office in befitting vestments, lifting up chaste hearts and holy hands." With this eloquence Newman explains the Presence of Christ on our altars linking it to "wheat-flour," "pure wine," "majestic words," "sacrificial rite," "altar," "sanctuary," "priests"—all of which stir reflection on the mystery of the Lord's Presence among us.

Newman captures the moment of transubstantiation in exquisite prose: "Jesus took bread, and blessed it, and made it His body; He took wine and gave thanks and made it His blood, and He gave His Apostles the power to do what He had done."

This for me is the best expression in English of this essential doctrine.

Is it any wonder that almost every word in this preceding explanation is monosyllabic? This powerful doctrine is directly and beautifully stated in thirty-five words, which are simple and direct, so that our faith may be likewise.

Then Newman explains the role of the priest: "Frail, ignorant, sinful man, but the sacerdotal power given to him compels the Presence of the Highest; he lays Him in a small tabernacle; he dispenses Him to a sinful people." The priest is frail; he is ignorant and sinful, doubtless. Yet by the power of priesthood he "compels the Presence of the Highest." He places God on the altar. Then he dispenses the Lord to a sinful people. And they receive Him. Some have just been cleansed from sin, some will return to it; the best of us and the worst of us will make the Lord our guest.

For Newman the Eucharist was not the *invocation* of God, calling on God. It was the *evocation* of God, calling Him forth, making Him present among us on the altar. This great action brings the eternal God to meet us.

Newman beautifully recognized the role of Mary and the Eucharist: "She receives Him to whom once she gave birth"—thus he describes the Blessed Mary at Mass and St. John celebrating (after the ascension). It was a time of bereavement and of consolation for our Lady and the writer expresses that in words affectionate and moving, reuniting Mary and St. John once more.

The presence of our Lord within him prompted this most beautiful prayer: "In Holy Communion, give me the grace of a cheerful heart, an even temper, sweetness, gentleness, and brightness of mind, as walking in Your light and by Your grace. I pray You to give me the spirit of over-abundant, ever-springing love, which overpowers and sweeps away the vexations of life by its own riches and strength and which above all things unites me to You who are the fountain and the center of all mercy, loving kindness and joy."

That Newman loved the Eucharist cannot be doubted, and his writing exudes that love triumphantly.

"To me nothing is so consoling, so piercing, so thrilling as the Mass.... I could attend Mass forever and not be tired."

"In Holy Communion give me the grace of a cheerful heart, an even temper, sweet-

ness, gentleness and brightness of mind, as walking in Your light and by Your grace. I pray You to give me the spirit of over-abundant, ever-springing love, which overpowers and sweeps away the vexations of life by its own riches and strength and which above all things unites me to You who are the fountain and the center of all mercy, loving kindness and joy."

Cardinal Newman

The Eucharist as Sacrament and Sacrifice

The Basic Teachings document of the National Conference of Catholic Bishops declares: "The Eucharist has primacy among the sacraments. It is of greatest importance for uniting and strengthening the Church. (The preceding chapters of this book have stressed the Eucharist as unity and strength especially.) The Eucharistic Celebration is carried out in obedience to the words of Jesus at the Last Supper. The words are: "Do this in remembrance of me."

At the same time that it is sacrifice, the Eucharist is a meal which recalls the Last Supper, celebrates our oneness in Christ and gives a foretaste of the banquet of the kingdom. Once we are nourished by the Lord we should eliminate all barriers to active love of our brothers. United with God, the sacrament joins us to each other.

As a *sacrament,* the Eucharist is the most excellent of all the sacraments: first in dignity, then in the grace it contains, and then in its permanency. It is a perfect sacrament when we receive it and when it is permanently retained in the tabernacles of our churches. The sacrament of the Eucharist is known under many other names: Blessed Sacrament, the real Bread of Life, the Sacrament of Life, Holy Communion and the Sacrament of Unity. All these express the truth and the essential meaning of the Eucharist as sacrament. All these reflect our Lord's desire to be one with us. St. Cyril says that we become through Communion "blood kindred of Jesus Christ." St. John Chrysostom says, "We are merged with Jesus." "Who shall separate me from the love of Jesus who is in me?" says St. Paul to the Romans (cf. 8:35).

Sacrifice is at the essence of all true religion. The Eucharist is also true *sacrifice,* a re-presentation of the sacrifice of Christ on the cross, for the ritual elements of the sacrifice are identical with the body and blood of Christ. The priest who offers the sacrifice is Christ and the victim is Christ. The sacrifice is not merely a ritual which commemorates a past sacrifice. In it, through the ministry of the priests, Christ perpetuates the sacrifice of the cross, but now in an unbloody manner. The very word Eucharist is derived from the Greek and means "good grace." It applies to this sacrifice of the new law in which Christ Himself is present, is offered, and is received under the species of bread and wine. Through the action of transubstantiation the entire Christ is made present in the Mass and that Presence is accomplished in the unbloody sacrifice. Jesus instituted this sacrifice as the first High Priest. He requested its repetition, and we know that the wish of Christ was fulfilled.

Vatican II teaches: "All (the laity's) work, prayers, and apostolic endeavors, their ordinary married and family life, their daily labor, their mental and physical relaxation, if carried out in the Spirit, and even the hardships of life, if patiently borne—all these become spiritual sacrifices acceptable through Jesus Christ." During the celebration of the Eucharist, these sacrifices are joined by us to the sacrifice of Christ on the cross and most lovingly offered to the Father.

Participation in this sacrifice is the source of one's Christian life. We offer the divine Victim to God and we offer ourselves along with the Victim.

The Presence of Christ in the sacrament derives from this sacrifice. Therefore, all devotion to the Blessed Sacrament draws us deeper into the notion of sacrifice. We offer our entire life with Christ to the Father in the Holy Spirit. For this we receive in exchange the wonderful gifts of faith, hope and love. We nourish the right dispositions by this devotion to celebrate this memorial of the Lord and to receive the Bread of Life, the Eucharist, as sacrifice and as sacrament.

"Receive Communion therefore! Eat the Bread of Life if you would live well, if you would obtain sufficient strength for the Christian combat, if you would possess happiness in the thick of misfortune" (St. Peter Julian Eymard).

"...Always bearing about in our body the mortification of Jesus, that the life of Jesus may be made manifest in our bodies" (cf. 2 Cor. 4:10).

O Jesus, present in the Blessed Sacrament, among the sacraments the Eucharist has primacy and is of the greatest power to unite and strengthen the Church. Accomplish this grace in our day.

The Eucharist and Pope John Paul II

In March, 1976, Cardinal Karol Wojtyla preached a series of conferences to Pope Paul VI and his co-workers. It is rare and probably unique for a Pope to have preached a retreat to one of his Predecessors. The theme of the conferences is mankind's encounter with and acceptance of Christ today. That theme was expressed by John Paul II in his inaugural address on October 22, 1978: "Brothers and sisters, do not be afraid to welcome Christ and accept His power. Open wide the doors for Christ. To His power open the boundaries of states, economic and political systems, the vast field of culture, civilization and development." The conferences are written with the Pontiff's characteristic simplicity and clarity. One treats of the Eucharistic Presence of Jesus. Here follow the essential points made by the Holy Father.

The Holy Father states: "The Church's principal means of sustenance is this sacramental action of the Eucharist in which the sacrifice and the constant presence of the Savior are manifested to the faithful." The Pope calls the Eucharist the principal means of sustenance in the Church, second therefore to none. He distinguishes the Eucharist as sacrifice and sacrament, which we have treated at greater length elsewhere in these pages.

The Pope discusses the power of Pentecost giving birth through the Holy Spirit to the new Church. The Church became a reality and her work of evangelization began. The Pope explains this Pentecost event by the quotation from Acts 1:8, "with the coming of the Holy Spirit you will receive the inner power to become witnesses to me." The Pope finds the power of Pentecost in the words of Jesus: "Do this in memory of me" (Lk. 22:19). These words said to the Apostles by Jesus give the power for the new evangelization of the Church.

The Apostles were then in the Upper Room as they were to be on the day of Pentecost. Jesus on Holy Thursday took the bread, broke it, and gave it to them saying, "This is my body offered in sacrifice for you" (1 Cor. 11:24) and then: "This is the cup of my blood for the new and everlasting covenant shed for you and for all men" (Lk. 22:20). The Lord added "Do this," thus forging the link between Himself and the action of the Apostles. "The link he forged lasts forever." Thus does the Holy Father explain the perpetuation of the Eucharistic institution in the Upper Room and its power to launch the Church. He discusses, therefore, the twofold power of the Eucharist and of Pentecost giving birth to the Church and vitality forever.

The Holy Father takes pains to state that Christ comes back not merely as a memory in the Eucharist, not merely someone written and talked about. But "I am" *"vere substantialiter, sacramentaliter"* (DS 883/1651), "I am the power from on high that shapes and sustains the Church, the community of the People of God."

The Eucharist, the Holy Father goes on to say, "is the gift of His Person, His action, conclusive, definitive and therefore saving action." The gift of the Eucharist is the gift of the bridegroom to the bride. Consequently, the Church, Bride of Christ, takes a new dimension in Christ.

The Pope says that the Eucharist is the principal source of all that is bestowed on the Church and on all men. "It is inexhaustible in its riches which pulsate in Christ."

"We are poor but we are rich. The Bridegroom is with you!" In a unique way Pope John Paul II shows the connection in the birth of the Church between the power of Christ in the Eucharist and the power of the Holy Spirit on Pentecost. Not just a then-and-gone power, but a here-and-now power all through the life of the Church.

The Bridegroom is with you!

O Jesus, present in the Blessed Sacrament, be the source of strength, of health, and of salvation to our beloved Pontiff, Pope John Paul II, that he may be a source of unity and strength to the flock committed to his care.

The Eucharist and Holy Thursday

On Holy Thursday the Lord instituted the most Blessed Sacrament: "No greater love." On Holy Thursday at the Last Supper He gave Himself *to* us. On the next day, Good Friday, He would give Himself *for* us on the cross.

I remember very vividly the Holy Thursdays when I was a boy. We used to look forward to this day as a spiritual starter for Easter. It was truly a day of holy remembrance of the Blessed Savior.

The Mass of Holy Thursday was always very well prepared for, especially by those of us who served at the altar. I remember so clearly the ringing of the bells at the *Gloria* and then the silence till the Easter resurrection, the sermon that reenacted the Last Supper, the washing of the feet of the Apostles—all brought you back to that moment in time when it actually happened. That was the only way to approach Holy Thursday, to relive the event. Then great crowds came to the altar to receive the Bread of Life, because this was the special day of the institution of the Eucharist. All was climaxed by the beautiful candlelight procession from the high altar, with the priest in gold cope carrying the monstrance as the altar boys incensed the sacrament. The congregation would then sing the *Pange Lingua* as the altar boys' procession made its way to the altar of repose, which had been lavishly and exquisitely bedecked with flowers to honor the sacrament. Then the silent, long vigil through the night, as thousands of adorers went from one church to another to adore at the repository of each. I remember that as children we tried to visit as many churches as possible in our city all through the night. In some churches we stood in line as the people passed before the repository admiringly and adoringly. At each repository altar we adored the Eucharist and we prayed for our dear ones. This was nothing extraordinary. It was part of the lives of most of us. We were only school children, but we had simple faith in the Eucharist, and the grace of God activated that faith. Holy Thursday was this day of faith and grace from morning till evening.

What was particularly thrilling to me as I grew older was that we were not the only ones going from church to church to kneel at the repository—children all over the world were doing the same thing at the same time. "May the Heart of Jesus in the most Blessed Sacrament be praised, adored, and loved, and at every moment in all the tabernacles of the world till the end of time." It was so moving to be part of this assembly. It was wonderful to have this special day given to us to rejoice in the inestimable gift.

On the evening of Holy Thursday the beloved Apostle John rested his head on the breast of Christ. Now Christ rests His head on the breasts of His friends, and that every day of our lives, if we so wish. On Holy Thursday we recognize the blessing of this Presence, an impression of security, as if we actually heard the Lord say: "It is I, do not be afraid."

I can still picture myself when I was a child remembering that moment of Christian history and reliving it. I can still remember kneeling there as a young man before the repository, and the longer I would kneel, the more difficult it would become to tear myself away. The contrast between the darkness of the church lighted only by candles and the glitter of the outside world struck me even then. Then I could hear: "And if I be lifted up,

I will draw all things to myself" (Jn. 12:32). The words pierced the silence. Yet they brought a tenderness to the day.

On Holy Thursday many lives are decided, many vocations take shape, I am sure. Many are called to the priesthood on that day. On Holy Thursday the plan of God for mankind, in the Eucharist is revealed and fulfilled. The plan of God for many other individuals who kneel before the Real Presence becomes known. On one Holy Thursday I came to realize that you never walk alone.

O Jesus, present in the Blessed Sacrament, Holy Thursday is a gift of Yourself to the Church.

May the Heart of Jesus in the most Blessed Sacrament be praised, adored, and loved at every moment in all the tabernacles of the world even to the end of time.

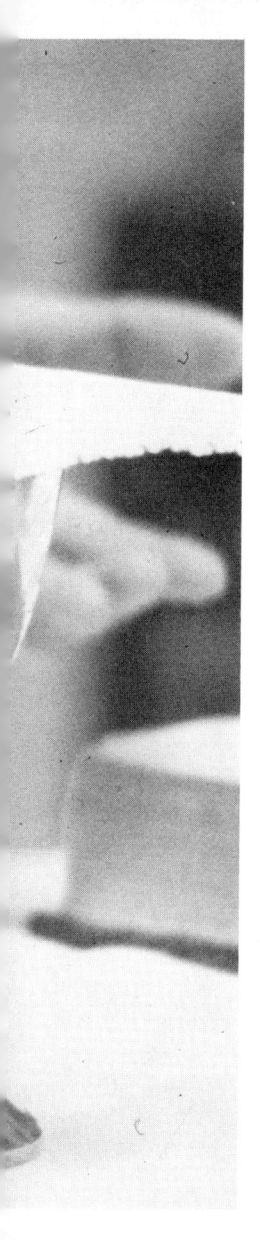

The Eucharist and the Priest

"Jesus took bread in His hands and blessed it and made it His body. He took wine and gave thanks and made it His blood. And He gave His Apostles the power to do what He had done" (Cardinal Newman, *Meditations and Devotions*). That was the institution not only of the Eucharist but also of Holy Orders, the sacrament of the priesthood. We must not let this institution of the Sacrament of the Eucharist obscure the gift of the priesthood.

From Christ the Priest comes the sacrament but He gave His Apostles the power to continue the sacramental presence. "Do this in memory of me" (Lk. 12:19). "Do this, as often as you drink it [the cup], in remembrance of me" (1 Cor. 11:25). The twelve Apostles are the first priests. The Apostles knew they were different from the rest of men. They had a special mission connected with the Eucharist. On them its continuance depended. They immediately replaced the fallen away Judas with Matthias. "And the lot fell upon Matthias, and he was numbered with the eleven Apostles" (Acts 1:26). God needs men. Until the end of the world, we shall need the grace of Holy Thursday. God knows that there will always have to be priests if we are going to have the Eucharist. Simultaneously Holy Thursday created the priesthood and the Eucharist. Now there is a scarcity of priests and the people are getting worried. It is a wonder that there are any priests, for, humanly speaking, they have little going for them—especially when you consider the indifference of the world to priests. It follows that the world will also be indifferent to the Eucharist, which is one with the priesthood. Too many do not believe in the power of the priesthood. Nor do they believe in the Presence of the Lord in the Eucharist. They are interrelated.

I often think of the many lonely villages across our country and across the world. In those lonely villages, (I have seen them in the less-Catholic-populated states) there is one small church, and one old priest kneeling in the sanctuary before the tabernacle. There he is the only adorer, and he must have great faith in the Eucharist, so strong that it can move mountains of indifference to the Eucharist and to him.

For hundreds of years, since the Holy Thursday institution, men have chosen to become priests. Better, God has chosen them. He will continue to do so, because He evangelized a world with twelve men, so numbers seem unimportant to God. "I will not leave you orphans" (Jn. 14:18). And besides, sins have to be forgiven—so there must be priests for many reasons.

We are among those chosen to succeed the Apostles. Only God knows why. 365 times a year for over thirty-eight years (12,870 times) I have acted in the place of Christ and said, "This is my body. This is my blood," more than the first half of the years in Latin, the latter decade or so in the vernacular. Always for me, God's most unworthy servant, with awe and trepidation. I mean this sincerely. But I hope I am what the Lord bargained for in choosing me as His instrument. We hold Christ in trembling hands and we kneel before the tabernacle with head held between our hands, lest, like Judas, we betray the Lord. We must pray to be worthy of the Eucharist, which we call down on the altar and dispense to the saints, the living saints of the Church. Some priests gave the Eucharist to St. Francis of Assisi and St. Theresa of Lisieux, to St. Teresa of Avila and to all the unknown saints. Today a priest gives the Eucharist to Mother Teresa and her sisters—how unworthy we would be of that privilege! We are not the Curé who spent hours in prayer at Ars before the Eucharist, especially before the crowds started to come. But the Lord still wants us to say Mass, to call people to the Eucharist.

Priests form an innumerable family—from St. John the Apostle until now, from St. Peter to John Paul II. The priesthood must be transmitted unto the end of time. Pray before the Eucharist for priests, that they be Eucharistic priests. Pray to the Eucharistic Jesus that there will be priests.

O Jesus, present in the Blessed Sacrament, give to the Church priests who are true adorers of the Eucharist, Eucharistic priests after the model of the Curé d'Ars, who spent so many hours in Your Presence for the sanctification of the clergy.

*The
Eucharist
and
Our Brethren*

How are we most closely united with Christ? Perhaps this beautiful story gives the answer:

Some thirty years ago, a priest was encouraging a group of refugees in a transit camp in Europe. "I do not know where any of you are going," he said. "But when you get there, go to the church, look for the sanctuary lamp, and then you will be at home."

Pope John Paul echoed these words when he spoke to the people of Guam:

"Where do we receive the impulse for being in true unity with Christ? *From the Eucharist,* for because there is one bread, we who partake of the bread are one body, the Body of Christ.

"My brothers and sisters, let us love one another in Christ!"

What the Holy Father asks of the people of Guam, he asks of us: that we deepen our faith in the Eucharistic Christ. This gives the power to transform the world, to help the brethren.

I heard of a mission bishop who said that it was difficult in his country to preach directly to non-Christians, but "the life of the faithful who live among them gives rise to inquiries about the Church, and conversions often follow." That life of the faithful is nourished by prayer and by faith in the Eucharist. When we make Jesus in the Eucharist the center of our lives, we do not turn away from people. We turn *toward* people and their needs —we are made more aware of all those who are members of the one body, the Body of Christ.

Through Eucharistic love and prayer, we become more sensitive to our brothers and sisters in distress. The poor children and the suffering become our children. On October 2, 1979, the Holy Father in his pastoral visit to the United States spoke from his heart when he said, "You must take of your substance and not just of your abundance to help them."

Faith in the Eucharist makes us see all men and women of all nations in the image of Christ. We recognize Christ in every human being. No man goes alone to God. In the Dogmatic Constitution on the

Church, November 21, 1964, no. 9, we read: "God does not make men holy and save them merely as individuals." The adoration of Jesus in the Eucharist is not an individually personal act; it joins us to the community of faith. That is how I see it—joining us to each other's lives. Eventually the visible Church on earth shall have made Christ in the Sacrament of the Eucharist present to every nation. Then the Church becomes progressively a sign of unity to all men. It becomes the salvation of all men. I do not think that anyone would doubt God's power to leaven the world through the Eucharist, through the institution of the Church. The whole world will be at home one day before the sanctuary lamp.

The missionary religious have many men and women of faith in the mission apostolate in the four corners of the earth. These same religious have central "motherhouses" where those stay who are not engaged in direct missionary work. They spend endless hours in prayer before the Eucharist, praying for those whose activity is almost ceaseless. In those same houses, especially at Masses said at dawn, even a person of little faith would feel the Eucharistic atmosphere of prayer. The Real Presence of the Lord on the altar becomes the strength of all the mission activity in this powerhouse. The Mass said in the small chapel transports us in thought to the first mission activity of the early Church. The perpetuity of Christianity is never more felt than in the Eucharist as it is adored in these circumstances. In these places even the coward becomes less aware of the allurements of the world and feels the strong creative silence of the Eucharist. He reaches out for his brother across the street and across the world.

> "Everything is silent. Do come, night of mine!
> Come hither, intangible shelter!
> Come, sacred nuptial silence. Come friendship!
> Come abundance!
> Come with me, come, my God,
> Come ardent repose!" — Paul Claudel

O Jesus, present in the Blessed Sacrament, through Eucharistic love and prayer make us more sensitive to our brothers and sisters in distress, that we will share with them the substance of our lives.

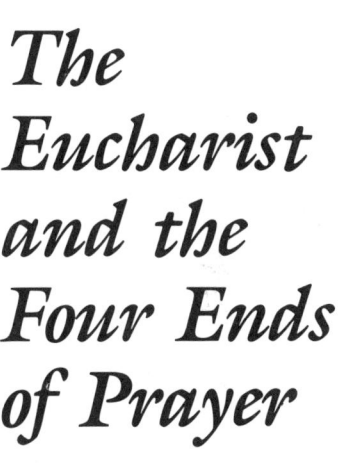

The Eucharist and the Four Ends of Prayer

No consideration of the Eucharist of this type could omit St. Alphonsus de Liguori, the founder of the Redemptorist congregation. He wrote his well-known *Visits to the Most Blessed Sacrament* in 1745. They immediately inflamed the hearts of men with a love of the Eucharist. No finer work is there to prepare us for the reception of Communion, to help us in the thanksgiving, and to provide prayerful helps for those who visit the Eucharistic God each day.

St. Alphonsus tells of a Spanish Poor Clare who loved to make long visits to the Blessed Sacrament. The other nuns asked what she did during those long silent hours. "I could kneel there forever," she answered. "And why not? God is there. You wonder what I do in the Presence of God. I marvel. I love. I thank. I beg."

Here is the essence of Eucharistic prayer. Here are the four ends of Eucharistic prayer. Under the guidance of

St. Alphonsus all of our time spent before the Eucharist can fall into the four categories, 1. adoration 2. thanksgiving 3. reparation and 4. petition. Every time I receive the Eucharist at Mass, this is my thanksgiving—perhaps just a few minutes at the altar adoring the Eucharistic Presence, thanking God for all His graces, telling the Lord of my sorrow for the sins of a lifetime, and begging Him for the graces and favors I need. We can also do this in the Holy Hour with a prolonged period for each segment. I know of no better informal structure or heart-to-heart arrangement for a visit to the Eucharist.

Modeling our prayer on the outline of St. Alphonsus, we recognize our littleness and adore the great God. "God is the great God and I am little I." We adore Jesus present in the living Bread in all tabernacles of the world.

We thank Jesus for all the wonderful graces and blessings of our lifetime. We thank Him for giving Himself to us in the most Blessed Sacrament. We thank Him for giving us His own Mother to be our Mother and for placing her by our side, *"Maria impende Juvamen."* We thank Jesus for our parents, our family, our friends, our home, our rearing in faith and love. We thank God for education, for vocation, for all these precious gifts. We could go on forever.

There is much to be sorry for, to offer reparation for. Just the disrespect that Jesus receives in the Sacrament from those who offend Him is enough. The places where Jesus is left abandoned and unloved—these cry for reparation. There are our personal sins, offenses, and negligence; our hardness of heart, our perdurance in sin. We are truly sorry. We want to be better. We promise to amend our lives. From now on, we give to the Lord our will, our love, our desires, everything we are and have.

We ask that God shower His love on us. We want to be faithful to the end of our lives. We ask to do the will of God exactly as God wants it done. We pray for those we love, the living and the dead, especially those who were close to Jesus and to Mary. We pray for the sinners, the deprived, the sick, the poor, the forgotten. We ask for the courage and strength of the Lord Himself. "Make us patient, kind and devoted to You and to Your work."

Thus we open our heart to the Lord with full confidence. We want to change after this audience with Jesus, each day of our lives. We want to amend our lives. We desire with much longing to please the

Lord, to know His will and to follow it perfectly. The wish of God is our command. If only we were willing to sacrifice everything to do the will of God! Some prefer many things to God. Each day we renew our resolution. Each day we determine good things for the future in our thanksgiving, petition, reparation and adoration. The ends of prayer to Jesus in the Eucharist are a good self-examination each day. They bring a new self-knowledge each day. They bring a new dependence on God and a new relationship to the Eucharist each day.

Thomas à Kempis says that we should speak to Christ in this Sacrament without fear, without formality: "as lover to his beloved, as friend to friend." The four ends of Eucharistic prayer facilitate this daily audience with Jesus.

"I could kneel there forever. And why not? God is there."   *A Spanish Poor Clare*

The Eucharist—Holy Communion

I constantly thank God that I was born a Catholic and that He has given us the grace of the Sacrament of the Eucharist. We know that the Eucharist is the heart and center of our Catholic Faith. It is good for us to be part of this Church, the true Church. The true Faith gives us the Bread of Life, which we must try to receive worthily, as worthily as human nature can.

We know well that we have numerous failings, much weakness, serious temptations of all kinds, and that this is part of all our lives for years and years. Yet Jesus tells us that He will help us and strengthen us through the Bread of Life.

"Come to me, all you who labor and are burdened, and I will give you rest."

"The bread that I will give is my flesh for the life of the world."

The frequent, even daily, reception of Holy Communion preserves us from living evil lives and helps and confirms us in a good life. The Eucharist is not a reward; it is a medicine for the sick. It is good for those who are hungry and seek strength. It gives that strength to fortify the soul. The Eucharist is food and nourishment par excellence. Therefore we should receive Holy Communion as often as possible. Then our disposition to receive will improve, not worsen through routine. We will then begin to lead a life which will make us more worthy to receive Holy Communion every day of our lives.

The dispositions to receive Holy Communion then will come directly from Jesus. They are a firm faith, a simple love, tranquillity of mind, zeal for souls, fervor, confidence and humility. Then will come still-increasing graces, as we receive the Eucharist more frequently. We begin to live solely for our Lord and solely through our Lord.

"Through him,
with him,
in him,
in the unity of the Holy Spirit,
all glory and honor is yours,
almighty Father,
for ever and ever. Amen" (Concluding Doxology, Eucharistic Prayer).

This is the best preparation for Holy Communion—to place Jesus at the center of our lives; to live for Him; to be obedient to His will always, not just when we feel like it.

"A te numquam separari permittas." "Never permit me to be separated from You." "Those things which please the Father, I do always."

The most important preparation is, then, to give our whole heart to Jesus without reservation. Only grave and sufficient reasons should keep us from Holy Communion. St. Augustine says that we must approach the holy table with our soul in the state of grace. We must strive for strong faith, hope and charity. We must have confidence in the good God. Our whole lives must be a preparation and a prolonged thanksgiving for each day's Communion.

Our whole lives become expressions of gratitude and love to Jesus Christ and then show to others His goodness and love in every action of the day.

More than anything, it is very important that we appreciate the Catholic Faith, that we believe in the Real Presence of Christ in the Blessed Sacrament, the Holy Sacrament of the altar. We cannot possibly penetrate this mystery. It is too profound, too beyond our ken. It is sufficient for us to believe that God can give us

Himself under the form of bread and wine and that He cannot deceive us. He would not deceive us.

I believe, my Lord and my God, that You are present in the Holy Eucharist. I believe that this Blessed Sacrament contains Your body, blood, soul and divinity, whole and entire under the appearance of bread. O my good Jesus, whom I adore here on earth by the light of faith, grant that I may one day adore You in the light of glory in heaven. Amen.

Daughters of St. Paul

IN MASSACHUSETTS
   50 St. Paul's Ave., Jamaica Plain, Boston, MA 02130;
     617-522-8911; 617-522-0875
   172 Tremont Street, Boston, MA 02111; **617-426-5464;**
     617-426-4230
IN NEW YORK
   78 Fort Place, Staten Island, NY 10301; **212-447-5071**
   59 East 43rd Street, New York, NY 10017; **212-986-7580**
   625 East 187th Street, Bronx, NY 10458; **212-584-0440**
   525 Main Street, Buffalo, NY 14203; **716-847-6044**
IN NEW JERSEY
   Hudson Mall — Route 440 and Communipaw Ave.,
     Jersey City, NJ 07304; **201-433-7740**
IN CONNECTICUT
   202 Fairfield Ave., Bridgeport, CT 06604; **203-335-9913**
IN OHIO
   2105 Ontario St. (at Prospect Ave.), Cleveland, OH 44115; **216-621-9427**
   25 E. Eighth Street, Cincinnati, OH 45202; **513-721-4838**
IN PENNSYLVANIA
   1719 Chestnut Street, Philadelphia, PA 19103; **215-568-2638**
IN VIRGINIA
   1025 King St., Alexandria, VA 22314 **703-683-1741**
IN FLORIDA
   2700 Biscayne Blvd., Miami, FL 33137; **305-573-1618**
IN LOUISIANA
   4403 Veterans Memorial Blvd., Metairie, LA 70002; **504-887-7631;**
     504-887-0113
   1800 South Acadian Thruway, P.O. Box 2028, Baton Rouge, LA 70821
     504-343-4057; 504-343-3814
IN MISSOURI
   1001 Pine Street (at North 10th), St. Louis, MO 63101; **314-621-0346;**
     314-231-1034
IN ILLINOIS
   172 North Michigan Ave., Chicago, IL 60601; **312-346-4228**
     312-346-3240
IN TEXAS
   114 Main Plaza, San Antonio, TX 78205; **512-224-8101**
IN CALIFORNIA
   1570 Fifth Avenue, San Diego, CA 92101; **714-232-1442**
   46 Geary Street, San Francisco, CA 94108; **415-781-5180**
IN HAWAII
   1143 Bishop Street, Honolulu, HI 96813; **808-521-2731**
IN ALASKA
   750 West 5th Avenue, Anchorage AK 99501; **907-272-8183**

IN CANADA
   3022 Dufferin Street, Toronto 395, Ontario, Canada
IN ENGLAND
   128, Notting Hill Gate, London W11 3QG, England
   133 Corporation Street, Birmingham B4 6PH, England
   5A-7 Royal Exchange Square, Glasgow G1 3AH, England
   82 Bold Street, Liverpool L1 4HR, England
IN AUSTRALIA
   58 Abbotsford Rd., Homebush, N.S.W., Sydney 2140, Australia